Kindergarten
domestic animals

KU-473-467

cat

cat

The cat is a small, furry animal, often kept as a pet. It has a small head, snout, strong jaws and sharp teeth. Cats have spongy footpads which enable them to walk quietly. The eyes of a cat seem to glow in the dark. Cats usually hunt for food.

dog

The dog is a part of the wolf family. Dogs are of two kinds — wild ones and pets. A dog is very intelligent, its intelligence varying, depending upon its breed. A dog is usually used to guard the house. The police use dogs to help them in their work. Dogs are also used to guide blind people and for herding sheep.

chicken

A chicken is a bird that is raised for its meat and eggs. There are probably more chickens than any other kind of bird, and they are found throughout the world. Chickens have claws on their feet. They use their claws and beaks as a defence against enemies, and also to dig in the soil for insects and seeds to eat.

rooster

A rooster is a male chicken with a beautiful red comb on his head, and a fleshy wattle under the beak which is bright red. Feathers cover most of its body, except for the lower legs and feet, which have scales. Roosters eat insects and seeds.

COW

A cow is a farm animal that feeds on grass, leaves, hay, twigs and fodder. Their colours vary from white, black and brown to tan. The male cow is called a bull. Its baby is called a calf. We get milk, butter, cheese and other dairy products from cows.

OX

Oxen have heavy bodies, long tails and divided hooves, and they chew their cud. Their smooth horns stand out from the side of the head, and are curved. They are powerful work animals and are used to carry heavy loads and pull carts.

donkey

Donkeys are suited to live in desert lands. They can live on lesser food than horses. If they eat more, they get sick. Donkeys have loud voices which they use to keep in touch with the rest of the herd. They have a powerful kick with which they defend themselves.

horse

The horse is a very useful animal that is suited for riding over long distances and for carrying loads. Horses have a good sense of smell, keen eyes, sharp ears and teeth. They eat only grain and grass. Horses are very intelligent and have a good memory.

goat

A goat is an important farm animal. Goats provide us with milk and meat. Some people keep goats as pets. Most goats have horns, which they use for fighting. An adult female goat is called a doe or nanny goat, and a baby goat is called a kid.

sheep

Sheep are important animals that provide us with wool, leather, milk and other products. Sheep walk on their hooves. They have strong legs and slim ankles which help them move quickly. They eat grass and can live without water for a long time.

rat

Rats are small, furry mammals that are found in all parts of the world. They have front teeth suited for gnawing; long, sharp claws and a slender, scaly tail. They are usually brown or black in colour. They eat almost any kind of plant or animal.

squirrel

A squirrel is a medium-sized rodent which lives in a nest called a drey that it makes in the branches of trees. Ground squirrels live on trees or under the ground. Flying squirrels have a special skin and can glide through the air. Squirrels often store food. They eat nuts, fruit, bark and leaves.

goose

A goose is a water bird which has a flattened bill, a long neck, waterproof feathers, long pointed wings, a short tail, short legs and webbed feet. Geese are larger than ducks and smaller than swans, and they honk. They are graceful in flight and can fly long distances without any rest.

duck

A duck is a bird with waterproof feathers and webbed feet. Ducks have short necks and wings and flat bills, and they quack or whistle. They are graceful on water, but waddle clumsily when walking on land. Ducks are raised for their meat.

camel

The camel is found in Africa, Asia and Australia. It usually lives up to 40 years. A male camel is called a bull; a female camel, a cow; and a baby camel, a calf or foal. A group of camels is called a herd. The camel is strong and can live without water or food for a long time in the desert. It stores its food in its hump.

llama

The llama looks like a small camel but without a hump. It has thick woolly fleece, and a long neck. Its fleece may be brown, buff, grey, white or black. The llama can carry heavy loads. If it is overloaded or tired, it will lie down and not move. When it is angry or under attack, it spits bad-smelling saliva in its enemy's face.

rabbit

The rabbit is a furry animal with long ears and a short, fluffy tail. Rabbits hop from place to place on their strong hind legs. They may be nice as pets, but farmers do not like them, because they eat up all the carrots and turnips. Rabbits are raised for their meat and fur.

hamster

A hamster is a small, chunky, furry rodent that has a short tail and large cheek pouches in which it can carry a lot of food. Hamsters have light reddish-brown fur on the back and white fur on the underside. They eat fruits, seeds, green vegetation, and some small animals.

quail

Quails are small birds. They live in open grasslands. They are grey or brown in colour. This makes them hard to spot and kill when they sit in the grass. Quails live in groups called coveys. Most quails can only fly for a short distance. They are often hunted for sport or food.

turkey

A turkey has a distinctive fleshy wattle that hangs from the underside of its beak. It is a brilliantly coloured bird that has eyelike spots on its tail. The hen is much smaller than the male (tom), and much less colourful. With their huge wings, turkeys are by far the largest birds on the farms.

parrot

A parrot is a colourful bird with red, green, blue or yellow feathers. They are popular pets as they can be easily tamed and taught to talk. Parrots have two toes that point backward and two that point forward. They have a curved beak. They eat fruits, seeds, nuts and berries.

canary

Canaries are bright yellow in colour and are often kept as pets because they are cheerful birds and sing beautifully. They build nests of dry moss and grass on the branches of trees. Every year, they change some of their songs.

pigeon

Pigeons fly at great speed. They are black, brown, blue or grey in colour. They have short and strong legs and stiff feathers. Some pigeons have a beautiful fan-shaped tail. Others have crowns of thin, lacy feathers. Pigeons eat grains, nuts and insects. They use their beaks like straws, to suck water.

budgerigar

Budgerigars are brightly-coloured birds with colourful feathers. They are clever and can be trained to talk. They can also be taught to do tricks. They make lovable pets. Male budgerigars have a blue patch of skin on their noses, while females have a brown patch. Budgerigars eat seeds and fruits.

yak

The yak is a large animal. It has a long, silky, brown-black hairy coat. Although it is so big, it can easily slide down icy slopes or swim in fast-flowing rivers. The yak is a useful animal. It gives milk and can carry heavy loads. Its fur is used to make woollen clothes.

monkey

Monkeys are very intelligent animals. Their bodies are suited to live in and around trees and they can climb, leap and run. Monkeys eat anything — eggs, flowers, frogs, fruits, insects, leaves, lizards, nuts and roots. Some people keep them as pets.

turtle

A turtle is a reptile with a hard shell.
Turtles can pull their heads, legs and tails
into their shells, which serve as a
protection. They like to live in water, so
most people keep them in glass tanks.
The shells of some turtles are plain black,
brown or green. But others may have
green, orange, red or yellow markings.